BECOMING
MOM
STRONG

Heidi St. John

TYNDALE
MOMENTUM™

The nonfiction imprint of
Tyndale House Publishers, Inc.

Welcome!

These empty pages are your future, soon to become your past. They will read the most personal tale you shall ever find in a book.

—*Anonymous*

WELCOME, DEAR MOM!

I am so glad you have decided to give journaling a try. I love journaling—but I have to confess, I'm not always good at it. Like me, you may love the idea of journaling and start off with great intentions, only to feel defeated and lose momentum when life does what it does best—change the plan. As a mother of seven, I've had my plans interrupted more times than I can count. Sound familiar?

There have been seasons in my journey as a mom when I've written in my journal every day. But there have also been times when days, weeks, or even an entire year has gone by while my journal just sat there, unloved and untouched. And do you know what? That's okay. After all, raising the next generation of teachers, doctors, pastors, judges, attorneys, and parents is an important and time-consuming job! But looking back, even the silence between those entries serves as a valuable reminder of the season I was in at the time. And that in itself is a gift I will cherish forever.

My point is, journaling is an activity that should bring you joy, regardless of how often you're able to do it. Even if you only write in your journal occasionally, I promise you the frustrations, fears, dreams, triumphs, and, yes, even the unspoken emotions you give words to now will become a treasured keepsake in the years to come.

As you start putting your thoughts onto the pages of this book, you'll soon discover a rhythm of your heart, expressed in prayers, stories, and even the unfinished sentences of a busy mom. This is your space, your canvas. Savor these moments of quiet (or not-so-quiet!) reflection. You're on an extraordinary journey, precious mom. It will be worth it to take the time to record the moments you just might otherwise forget about along the way.

I'll be praying for you!

—Heidi St. John

A Few Tips for Successful Journaling

— Keep your journal where you'll use it most. A dear friend of mine keeps hers by her bed, and for a few years I kept mine in my diaper bag, because I never knew when I'd have a free moment in the car or at a doctor's appointment.

— Try to write when you're least distracted. Quiet time is a friend to moms who are trying to sort out their thoughts and feelings.

— Don't beat yourself up when the days get away from you. There were many times when a baby had kept me up all night and my journal entry said, "Would rather be sleeping!"

— Write whatever comes to mind. It may be a special interaction you had with your child that day or an unexpected moment that you don't want to forget.

— Be real. Your journal should reflect the real you—flaws and all. When I look back over years of journal entries, slow heart changes become evident. Growth in my marriage, my mothering, and even my dependence on God show up with greater clarity over time. Yours will too!

— Date each entry. Looking back, you'll see that God's timing is perfect. He never does anything without your good in mind.

— Highlight answers to prayer. These answers can be forgotten in the day-to-day hustle of life. When we write them down, they become precious reminders that God can be trusted with future problems too.

— Record your favorite verses or quotes that encourage you. Remember, your children may read your journals one day! What encourages you will encourage them, too!

— Write about your children—their growth in the Lord, their struggles, and answers to your prayers for them.

— Write about your marriage. Sometimes it's the little moments that end up making the biggest impact. Every marriage has its ups and downs. Times spent writing prayers for your husband can become precious moments of remembrance in years to come.

Fill your paper with the breathings of your heart.

— William Wordsworth

The very essence of your words is truth;
all your just regulations will stand forever.

— *Psalm 119:160*

God never wastes anything.

—*HSJ*

Make them holy by your truth; teach
them your word, which is truth.

— *John 17:17*

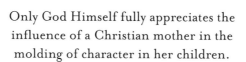

Only God Himself fully appreciates the
influence of a Christian mother in the
molding of character in her children.

— *Billy Graham*

Lead me by your truth and teach me,
for you are the God who saves me. All
day long I put my hope in you.

— *Psalm* 25:5

Prayer is not asking. Prayer is putting oneself
in the hands of God, at his disposition, and
listening to his voice in the depths of our hearts.

— Mother Teresa

Teach me your ways, O Lord, that I may
live according to your truth! Grant me
purity of heart, so that I may honor you.

— *Psalm 86:11*

We can say with confidence, "The LORD
is my helper, so I will have no fear.
What can mere people do to me?"

— *Hebrews 13:6*

*No matter what we face, God is our help. He is also the
one we can count on to help our children. Have you taken
your fears to the Lord today? He wants to help you.*

— *HSJ*

Letting go isn't giving up. It's trusting
God to do whatever He has to do.

— *Francine Rivers*

Don't turn your back on wisdom, for she will
protect you. Love her, and she will guard you.
Getting wisdom is the wisest thing you can do!
And whatever else you do, develop good judgment.

— Proverbs 4:6-7

Courage comes from a heart that
is *convinced* it is loved.

— Beth Moore

For the LORD your God is living among you.
He is a mighty savior. He will take delight in you
with gladness. With his love, he will calm all your
fears. He will rejoice over you with joyful songs.

— Zephaniah 3:17

The hand that rocks the cradle
is the hand that rules the world.

— W. R. Wallace

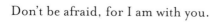

Don't be afraid, for I am with you.

— *Isaiah 41:10*

I have been driven many times upon my knees
by the overwhelming conviction that I had
nowhere else to go. My own wisdom and that of
all about me seemed insufficient for that day.

— *Abraham Lincoln*

The LORD is my light and my salvation—
so why should I be afraid? The LORD
is my fortress, protecting me from
danger, so why should I tremble?

— *Psalm 27:1*

A wise woman builds her home, but a foolish
woman tears it down with her own hands.

— *Proverbs* 14:1

*Do my priorities at home reflect God's heart
for my family? Is what I'm doing right now
building my home or tearing it down?*

— HSJ

Enjoy the little things, for one day you may
look back and realize they were the big things.

— *Robert Brault*

"For I know the plans I have for you," says the LORD. "They are plans for good and not for disaster, to give you a future and a hope."

— *Jeremiah 29:11*

When I stand before God at the end of
my life, I would hope that I would not
have a single bit of talent left, and could
say, "I used everything you gave me."

— Erma Bombeck

Come to me, all of you who are weary and
carry heavy burdens, and I will give you rest.
Take my yoke upon you. Let me teach you,
because I am humble and gentle at heart,
and you will find rest for your souls.

— *Matthew 11:28-29*

a MOM
STRONG
MOM
KNOWS
WHAT
SHE'S
fighting for

Grace is a love that rescues. It is
peace in the midst of pain.

—HSJ

He gives power to the weak and
strength to the powerless.

—Isaiah 40:29

The more you pray, the less you'll panic.
The more you worship, the less you worry.
You'll feel more patient and less pressured.

—Rick Warren

Wait patiently for the LORD. Be brave and
courageous. Yes, wait patiently for the LORD.

—Psalm 27:14

How joyful are those who fear
the LORD—all who follow his ways!

—*Psalm 128:1*

*Struggling with the many sometimes "unseen" parts of
motherhood? Take a step back and try to see your children
five, ten, even twenty years from now. God promises
that happiness is one of the things we can count on as we
walk in his ways and teach our children to do the same.*

—*HSJ*

If our children have the background of a godly, happy home, and this unshakable faith that the Bible is indeed the Word of God, they will have a foundation that the forces of hell cannot shake.

—Ruth Bell Graham

And we know that God causes everything to work together for the good of those who love God and are called according to his purpose for them.

—*Romans 8:28*

Making the decision to have a child is momentous. It is to decide forever to have your heart go walking around outside your body.

—Elizabeth Stone

No eye has seen, no ear has heard, and
no mind has imagined what God has
prepared for those who love him.

—*1 Corinthians 2:9*

a **MOM**
STRONG
MOM
has courage
& TRUSTS
IN THE
LORD

The trail is the thing, not the end
of the trail. Travel too fast and you
miss all you are traveling for.

—Louis L'Amour

Let all that I am wait quietly before God, for my hope is in him. He alone is my rock and my salvation, my fortress where I will not be shaken. My victory and honor come from God alone. He is my refuge, a rock where no enemy can reach me. O my people, trust in him at all times. Pour out your heart to him, for God is our refuge.

—*Psalm 62:5-8*

Perfection isn't what matters. In fact, it's the
very thing that can destroy you if you let it.

—*Emily Giffin*

The faithful love of the LORD never ends! His
mercies never cease. Great is his faithfulness;
his mercies begin afresh each morning.

Lamentations 3:22-23

I am leaving you with a gift—peace of mind and heart. And the peace I give is a gift the world cannot give. So don't be troubled or afraid.

—*John 14:27*

God doesn't work like the world works. Aren't you glad? When He says He will give you peace, you can trust Him. Are you allowing your troubled heart to be at peace and trust in God's promise today?

—*HSJ*

Down through the years, I turned to the
Bible and found in it all that I needed.

—Ruth Bell Graham

I am the LORD, and I do not change.

—*Malachi* 3:6

Who we are and how we engage with the world are
much stronger predictors of how our children
will do than what we know about parenting.

—Brené Brown

Whatever is good and perfect is a gift coming
down to us from God our Father, who
created all the lights in the heavens.

—*James 1:17*

a **MOM**
STRONG
MOM
is not defined
BY HER
PAST

I can shake off everything if I write;
my sorrows disappear; my courage is reborn.

—Anne Frank

But you are always the same; you will live forever.

—*Psalm 102:27*

When you feel like you're failing, look up!

—HSJ

Direct your children onto the right path,
and when they are older, they will not leave it.

—*Proverbs 22:6*

Can a mother forget her nursing child? Can she feel no love for the child she has borne?

—*Isaiah 49:15*

Just like we could never abandon or forget our nursing infant, God would never abandon or forget us. He sees whatever you are facing right now. Be encouraged! You are loved, precious mom.

—*HSJ*

The impression that a praying mother
leaves upon her children is life-long.

—D. L. Moody

Now may the God of peace—who brought
up from the dead our Lord Jesus, the great
Shepherd of the sheep, and ratified an eternal
covenant with his blood—may he equip you
with all you need for doing his will. May he
produce in you, through the power of Jesus
Christ, every good thing that is pleasing to him.
All glory to him forever and ever! Amen.

—*Hebrews 13:20-21*

At the end of the day, the enemy is going to be
sorry he ever messed with you. You're about to
become his worst nightmare a million times over.
He thought he could wear you down, sure that
after a while you'd give up without much of a fight.
Well, just wait till he encounters the fight of God's
Spirit in you. Because . . . This. Means. War.

—Priscilla Shirer

I could have no greater joy than to hear that
my children are following the truth.

—3 John 1:4

a **MOM**
STRONG
MOM
is not afraid
TO STAND UP
FOR WHAT
SHE
BELIEVES IN

Life appears to me too short to be spent in
nursing animosity or registering wrongs.

— *Charlotte Brontë*

I will teach all your children, and
they will enjoy great peace.

—*Isaiah* 54:13

There are two ways of spreading light: to be
the candle or the mirror that reflects it.

—Edith Wharton

Be still, and know that I am God!

—*Psalm* 46:10

I will comfort you there in Jerusalem
as a mother comforts her child.

—*Isaiah 66:13*

*Motherhood has many seasons. Up all night with a
new baby? Tired of toddler taming? Exhausted from
an ongoing battle with a wayward child? God knows
what it's like. He wants to comfort you in the same way
you bring comfort to your children. He is so good!*

—*HSJ*

Motherhood is tough. If you just want a wonderful
little creature to love, you can get a puppy.

—Barbara Walters

Those who live in the shelter of the Most High
will find rest in the shadow of the Almighty.

—*Psalm 91:1*

We become what we purpose to become—
what we're intentional about becoming.

—HSJ

Don't worry about anything; instead, pray
about everything. Tell God what you need,
and thank him for all he has done.

—*Philippians 4:6*

We can do no great things—only
small things with great love.

—Mother Teresa

Above all, clothe yourselves with love, which
binds us all together in perfect harmony.

—*Colossians 3:14*

The loveliest masterpiece of the heart
of God is the heart of a mother.

— St. Therese of Lisieux

Since we are living by the Spirit, let us follow
the Spirit's leading in every part of our lives.

—*Galatians 5:25*

Mary responded, "Oh, how my soul praises the Lord. How my spirit rejoices in God my Savior! For he took notice of his lowly servant girl, and from now on all generations will call me blessed."

—*Luke 1:46-48*

We can learn so much from the mother of Jesus. Even upon hearing what was probably frightening news, she chose to lift her heart to God in prayer. Mary reminds us that when we turn our hearts heavenward, blessing is sure to follow—even generational blessing!

—*HSJ*

You are never too old to set another
goal or to dream a new dream.

—C. S. Lewis

Don't be selfish; don't try to impress others.
Be humble, thinking of others as better than
yourselves. Don't look out only for your own
interests, but take an interest in others, too.

—Philippians 2:3-4

Becoming a mother makes you the mother
of all children. From now on each wounded,
abandoned, frightened child is yours.
You live in the suffering mothers of every
race and creed and weep with them. You
long to comfort all who are desolate.

—*Charlotte Gray*

O people, the LORD has told you what is good, and
this is what he requires of you: to do what is right,
to love mercy, and to walk humbly with your God.

—Micah 6:8

a **MOM STRONG MOM KNOWS WHAT** *true beauty is*

Your kids don't need you to be perfect.
They need you to be present.

—HSJ

God blesses those who are persecuted for doing
right, for the Kingdom of Heaven is theirs.

—*Matthew 5:10*

God is the God of "right now." He doesn't
want you sitting around regretting yesterday.
Nor does He want you wringing your hands
and worrying about the future. He wants
you focusing on what He is saying to you and
putting in front of you . . . right now.

—Priscilla Shirer

When she speaks, her words are wise,
and she gives instructions with kindness.

—*Proverbs 31:26*

Standing near the cross were Jesus' mother, and
his mother's sister, Mary (the wife of Clopas),
and Mary Magdalene. When Jesus saw his mother
standing there beside the disciple he loved, he said
to her, "Dear woman, here is your son." And he
said to this disciple, "Here is your mother." And
from then on this disciple took her into his home.

— John 19:25-27

Jesus values the role you and I have as mothers. He
sees the struggle and appreciates every unseen thing
you do to care for your children each day. Even
more than that—he beautifully demonstrates how we
should treat mothers. Moms are precious to God.

—HSJ

Mothers and their children are in a category all their own. There's no bond so strong in the entire world. No love so instantaneous and forgiving.

—Gail Tsukiyama

From a wise mind comes wise speech;
the words of the wise are persuasive.

—*Proverbs 16:23*

One of the things they never tell you about
child raising is that for the rest of your life,
at the drop of a hat, you are expected to know
your child's name and how old he or she is.

—Erma Bombeck

The LORD grants wisdom! From his mouth
come knowledge and understanding.

—*Proverbs 2:6*

a MOM STRONG MOM

has hope

IN TIMES OF SORROW

There is more power in a mother's
hand than in a king's scepter.

—Billy Sunday

Fear of the LORD is the foundation of true wisdom. All who obey his commandments will grow in wisdom. Praise him forever!

—*Psalm 111:10*

You can learn many things from children.
How much patience you have, for instance.

—Franklin P. Jones

True wisdom and power are found in God;
counsel and understanding are his.

— *Job 12:13*

_____

_____

_____

_____

_____

_____

_____

_____

_____

_____

Honor your father and mother. Then
you will live a long, full life in the land
the LORD your God is giving you.

—*Exodus 20:12*

God holds mothers in high regard, and instructs
others to do the same. Are you honoring your
parents? Are you teaching your children to honor
their parents? Blessing follows those who honor
their parents. It's a promise you can count on!

—*HSJ*

Motherhood: All love begins and ends there.

—Robert Browning

Joyful are people of integrity,
who follow the instructions of the LORD.

—*Psalm 119:1*

God has placed you right here, right now,
for such a time as this—to help prepare your
children for the battle that lies ahead!

—HSJ

[The LORD] grants a treasure of common
sense to the honest. He is a shield to
those who walk with integrity.

—Proverbs 2:7

Those who believe they can do something and those who believe they can't are both right.

—Henry Ford

May integrity and honesty protect
me, for I put my hope in you.

—*Psalm* 25:21

When we do the best that we can, we
never know what miracle is wrought in
our life, or in the life of another.

—*Helen Keller*

Get rid of all bitterness, rage, anger, harsh
words, and slander, as well as all types of evil
behavior. Instead, be kind to each other,
tenderhearted, forgiving one another, just
as God through Christ has forgiven you.

—*Ephesians 4:31-32*

Charm is deceptive, and beauty does not last; but a woman who fears the LORD will be greatly praised.

—*Proverbs 31:30*

It's easy to be distracted from following Jesus when we see "perfect" moms on magazine covers and Pinterest, isn't it? Remember that there is no such thing as the "perfect Proverbs 31" woman. God says that ultimately, our worth comes from Him. Pursuit of temporary things is just that: temporary. Enjoy beauty and accomplishment, but be on guard! Don't let those things become an idol. Keep your eyes on Jesus.

—*HSJ*

What we are is God's gift to us. What
we become is our gift to God.

—Eleanor Powell

Since God chose you to be the holy people he loves, you must clothe yourselves with tenderhearted mercy, kindness, humility, gentleness, and patience. Make allowance for each other's faults, and forgive anyone who offends you. Remember, the Lord forgave you, so you must forgive others.

—*Colossians 3:12-13*

I learned more about Christianity from my mother
than from all the theologians in England.

—John Wesley

If you forgive those who sin against you,
your heavenly Father will forgive you.

—*Matthew 6:14*

Set time aside to listen for that still small
voice. It's tempting to hurry, but trust me,
wisdom is worth wating for, and waiting on
God's direction is never a waste of time.

—HSJ

No one can make you feel inferior
without your consent.

—*Eleanor Roosevelt*

I will never fail you. I will never abandon you.

—Hebrews 13:5

You have enemies? Good. That means you've
stood up for something, sometime in your life.

—*Winston Churchill*

_____

_____

_____

_____

_____

_____

_____

_____

_____

_____

_____

_____

_____

_____

Be on guard. Stand firm in the faith.
Be courageous. Be strong.

—1 Corinthians 16:13

If you're feeling tired or inadequate today, get ready to find new strength.

JOIN HEIDI ST. JOHN AS SHE ENCOURAGES WOMEN TO
BECOME MOMSTRONG TOGETHER!

BECOMING MOMSTRONG

Heidi St. John brings women back to God's Word as the ultimate source for purpose and strength. Through her personal experiences and biblical truth, she shows her readers that they have the power of God at their disposal and that He has equipped them "for such a time as this" (Esther 4:14).

BECOMING MOMSTRONG BIBLE STUDY

God has provided a blueprint for becoming MomStrong, and that blueprint is found in the Bible. He has entrusted mothers to bring up the next generation, and He says His strength is made perfect in weakness. This six-week study will help mothers find their purpose and their strength in Christ.

BECOMING MOMSTRONG JOURNAL

Mothers can strengthen their hearts and souls by spending time with God, reflecting on what He has done, and growing a deeper faith they can pass on to their children. This beautifully designed companion journal to Heidi St. John's book *Becoming MomStrong* will be a helpful guide on the journey.

CP1264